PLATFORM PAPERS

QUARTERLY ESSAYS ON
THE PERFORMING ARTS

No. 25
October 2010

CURRENCY HOUSE

PLATFORM PAPERS
Quarterly essays from Currency House Inc.

Editor: Dr John Golder, j.golder@unsw.edu.au

Currency House Inc. is a non-profit association and resource centre advocating the role of the performing arts in public life by research, debate and publication.

Postal address: PO Box 2270, Strawberry Hills, NSW 2012, Australia
Email: info@currencyhouse.org.au   Tel: (02) 9319 4953
Website: www.currencyhouse.org.au   Fax: (02) 9319 3649

Editorial Board: Katharine Brisbane AM, Dr John Golder, John McCallum, Martin Portus, Greig Tillotson

Moving Across Disciplines: Dance in the 21st century copyright © Eric Brannigan, 2010

ISBN 978-0-9807982-1-0
ISSN 1449-583X
Typeset in 10.5 Arrus BT
Printed by Ligare Book Printers, Riverwood, NSW

SIDNEY MYER FUND

This edition of Platform Papers is supported by the Sidney Myer Fund, Neil Armfield, David Marr, Joanna Murray-Smith, Martin Portus, Alan Seymour and other individual donors and advisers. To them and to all our supporters Currency House extends sincere gratitude.

Contents

AVAILABILITY *Platform Papers*, quarterly essays on the performing
arts, is published every January, April, July and October and is
available through bookshops or by subscription. For order form,
see page 62.

LETTERS Currency House invites readers to submit letters of
400–1,000 words in response to the essays. Letters should be
emailed to the Editor at info@currencyhouse.org.au or posted to
Currency House at PO Box 2270, Strawberry Hills, NSW 2012,
Australia. To be considered for the next issue, the letters must be
received by 30 November.

CURRENCY HOUSE For membership details, see our website at:
www.currencyhouse.org.au

Moving Across Disciplines:

Dance in the twenty-first century

ERIN BRANNIGAN

The author

Dr Erin Brannigan works in the fields of dance and film as an academic, curator and journalist. She has been involved in the Australian dance community for over 20 years.

She trained in dance at Bodenwieser Dance Centre in Sydney and worked commercially as a dancer before studying Fine Arts at Sydney University. Erin has also worked in an administrative capacity in the performing arts for Performance Space, Onextra and Force Majeure.

Erin was the founding director in 1999 of the biennial ReelDance International Dance on Screen Festival and has curated dance screen programs and exhibitions for the Melbourne International Arts Festival (2003), the Sydney Festival (2008), for Dancehouse in Melbourne and Performance Space in Sydney, as well as several international dance screen festivals.

Erin writes on dance for the Australian arts newspaper, *RealTime*, and has been published in *Writings on Dance*, *Senses of Cinema* and the *International Journal of Performance Arts and Digital Media*.

Her PhD thesis is to be published later this year by Oxford University Press as *Dancefilm: Choreography and the Moving Image*. Her current project, on Australian choreographers, is a collaboration with *RealTime*, and includes new writing from dance theorists on local artists. She taught film studies and dance theory at Sydney University and the University of New South Wales, before taking up a position at the latter as Lecturer in Dance.

Acknowledgements

First, my thanks to Lucy Guerin, Helen Herbertson and Gideon Obarzanek for their generosity in sharing so much of their process and thinking with me in the interviews upon which this essay hinges and for graciously allowing me to cite them here. As always, it is the artists who inspire and challenge me to find the words to engage with them and their work.

I also thank Julie-Anne Long, Martin Del Amo and Sue Healey for their expertise, time and support in working through with me some of the central concerns in this paper, and Nalina Wait for her research support and advice. The members of the newly-formed Writing Dancing group were also very understanding, and at a recent meeting helped me sift through my rambling thoughts. I look forward to the opportunity to return the favour. And while I am at it, I should acknowledge the broader dance community in Sydney, who, against all the odds, fight on and continue to make things happen.

Thanks to Briony Trezise for her attentive reading of my text and succinct advice, and to Tere O'Connor, who came along with some radical and brilliant insights just when they were needed. I would also like to thank Elizabeth Dempster and Ramsay Burt, whose scholarship continues to be so valuable to me. And, of course, many thanks to 'the great John Golder', as he is known amongst students at UNSW, both for the opportunity to write this essay, and for his patience, understanding and insights throughout the process.

I would like to acknowledge the support of the Faculty of Arts and Social Sciences at UNSW, who awarded me an Early Career Researcher Grant for the larger project of which this Platform Paper is a part.

Finally, thanks to my friends and family for support through the often difficult writing periods, especially Mum and Dad for the babysitting; to Joe, Sunny and Billy, who have tolerated my long nights at the computer; and, last but not least, our latest addition, Hunny the Bunny, who kept my lap warm in the last few days.

Introduction

'The Spectre of Interdisciplinarity'

'Dance [...] as an arts practice [...] is but a pimple on the corpus of dance as human activity. It is a pimple in terms of its scale, its arrival, and the fact that its permanence is by no means guaranteed.'

Andrew Morrish[1]

For nearly half a century there has been discussion in the visual and performing arts regarding the tension between disciplinary specificity and a growing tendency towards 'multi-disciplinary' approaches to creating work. 'More than a decade has passed', wrote Rosalind Krauss and Annette Michelson back in 1979,

since the stability and coherence of the aesthetic field, as well as its continuity with its past, were disrupted by artistic practice which resists the reified and reifying categories (painting, sculpture, architecture, etc.), according to which art has traditionally been recognized, classified, and assimilated.[2]

Thirty years later, new categories of creative work include video art, body art, dance theatre, dance screen, physical theatre, verbatim theatre, interactive installations ... The list of hybrid terms continues to expand. Today, stability and coherence are challenged at just about every level, and that includes programming, funding and training.

At the beginning of the twenty-first century, contemporary dance is an interdisciplinary art form. It has found currency with progressive critical theories engaging new concepts of mobility and movement, and choreography is figured as a major player in informing and realising new understandings of key philosophical concepts.[3] The art form itself is in deep dialogue with experimental practices in new media, theatre, film and the visual arts, exploring shared and divergent knowledges and compositional strategies. Dance has emerged as a major player in contemporary performance practice, along with an expanded concept of *mise en scène* that is driven by new techniques and technologies.

In Europe and the Americas this trend is exemplified by the Belgian Alain Platel (who founded Les Ballets de la C de la B) and Brussels-based American choreographer Meg Stuart, choreographer William Forsythe and the New York City-based performance Group Troika Ranch, and dancer-choreographers, Michael Clark and Javier Frutos, from Scotland and Venezuela/UK respectively. The practice of these artists brings dance together with theatre (Platel and Stuart), with new media and film (Forsythe and Troika Ranch) and with design (Clark and De Frutos). But the same patterns of interdisciplinarity have been emerging here in Australia over at least the past 25 years, during which time I have been involved with the local and national dance scene as a writer, academic and curator. Larger dance companies such as Australian Dance Theatre and Melbourne-based Chunky Move are investing creative energy in interactive, imaging and robotic technologies, while independent choreographer Shelley Lasica, who has been working in gallery contexts since the mid-1980s continues her engagement with the visual arts field. Melbourne-based choreographer Lucy Guerin explores stage design as installation, and Helen Herbertson (ex-director of Dance Works and Dancehouse in Melbourne) invests in a partnership with designer Ben Cobham that also emphasizes the moving body as a component of a tightly constructed and staged *mise en scène*. Other partnerships include Melbourne choreographer Ros Warby's collaboration with lighting designer and filmmaker Margie Medlin; Kate Champion's work with designer Geoff Cobham for her Sydney-based company Force Majeure; Malaysian-Australian choreographer Tony Yap's exchange with musicians Tim Humphries and Madeleine Flynn, and video artist Samuel James' creative projects with a number of Sydney-based choreographers including Tess De Quincey, Julie-Anne Long and Narelle Benjamin. As often as not, the work resulting from these encounters and collaborations finds common ground at a conceptual level, so that 'separate data, concepts, theories, and methods' produce an interdisciplinary response to a central question or idea, to borrow from a generic definition of the term.[4] A feature shared by all these diverse performance practices is the challenge, first to the central role of language, and then to the emphasis placed by mainstream work on linearity and closure. But these challenges are mounted by the whole broad field of contemporary performance. Why single out dance? That is the question to which I shall presently return.

That dance does have an important place in these experimental collaborations is nothing new for a form that is almost defined by (and named after) its 'currency', whether in relation to epoch-defining ideas or radical shifts in other disciplines. To set this train of thought in motion, we only need to think of Merce Cunningham's engagement with Zen philosophy; John Cage's experimental music theories and 'neo-Dadaism' in the visual arts in the 1950s and '60s; or Yvonne Rainer's tussle with minimalism and anticipation of the celebrated feminist critique of the 'gaze' in Film Studies through her work in the 1960s and '70s. Starting each new production from scratch with limited pre-existing materials and the basic formal elements of movement, time, space and the body, dance seems to attract—and, moreover, seems well able to accommodate—other modes and other media. In an interview with me in June this year, Helen Herbertson went further: 'You can't deny the fact that [dance] really does love working with other forms. [...I]t's one of the few forms that can apply itself to sound or image.' It is this openness that has led to contemporary dance becoming intimately associated with some of the most interesting experiments and developments in the broader performance field. As dance theorist Ramsay Burt has written, in an article entitled 'The Spectre of Interdisciplinarity', 'Theater dance is an interdisciplinary form, and some of the most interesting advances in progressive and experimental dance work in recent years have been interdisciplinary in nature.'[5] Burt's use of the term 'theater dance' here distinguishes dance as a contemporary art form from social and traditional dance, suggesting an historical continuity regarding interdisciplinarity from its emergence at the turn of the century to the present—something for which I also want to argue.

4

The tendency toward interdisciplinarity in current creative practice is keenly felt by the dance community. One trajectory in the history of dance might be seen as leading from an integration with music, ritual and theatre in traditional forms (indigenous, Eastern, ballet), to 'pure movement' in Western theatre dance, initiated by Isadora Duncan and peaking with the mind/body practices that emerged from American university campuses in the 1960s. These US developments had parallels elsewhere and coincided with the emergence of a critical discourse that legitimised dance as a discrete field of inquiry, practice and performance, along with the institution of dance as an appropriate subject for study at tertiary level. This recognition appeared to be late in coming and hard won, but considering that Western theatre dance might be a twentieth-century phenomenon, perhaps the timing was just about right.

This is a radical way of looking at things—but it is the central provocation of this essay. To understand the disciplinary isolation of dance as a twentieth-century blip in a history of integrated performance practice is to oversimplify dramatically the history of a form that is hardly less complex and diverse than humanity itself. It is to conveniently overlook important distinctions between practice and performance, ritual, social and theatrical dance, physical therapy and choreographic exploration. But the questions I will focus on do require some sweeping gestures: *Does Australian contemporary dance practice exemplify interdisciplinarity? How are shifting disciplinary parameters impacting on choreographic research, pedagogy and critical discourse? And how is the radical interdisciplinarity of choreography changing the position of dance within the broader cultural ecology?*

What this contextualising of current practice *does* do is link contemporary dance back to pre-twentieth century practices, challenging Krauss and Michelson's notion of late twentieth-century interdisciplinarity as a break with the past—at least as far as dance is concerned. The work of the Ballets Russes, particularly at their most experimental while collaborating with the Futurists in Rome, is one historical precedent. But we can go even further back, to the earliest emergence of what would become classical ballet or the centuries-old form of Indian Kathak dance, in which choreography is only one component of a theatrical spectacle that encompasses ritual, storytelling, mimicry and music. Now, as then, dance and choreography can operate as one element in a performance event that moves across disciplinary specialisations, perhaps at one moment highlighting one, but then dissolving clear boundaries the next.

What is at stake here is the identity of a discipline that has struggled for recognition and legitimacy in a world dominated by the knowledges and authority of language. As somatic or corporeally-based knowledge, the art of dance has been marginalised politically, financially, theoretically and culturally. Yet its essential corporeality is both its major asset and defining feature. Dance theorist Mark Franko articulates the disciplinary dilemma neatly:

> Dance in its various manifestations as teaching, performance, and intellectual work seems to strain against the limitations of a narrowly defined disciplinary endeavour, while still attempting to conserve what distinguishes dance from other disciplines— that is, what makes dance itself a discipline.[6]

This disciplinary *unease* is reiterated in Herbertson's observation that the essential characteristic of 'physical specificity' that defines the form is also in danger of becoming simply a 'tool' for other art forms to use. Her comment that she is 'waiting for a kind of re-flowering of really specific, detailed physical language', discloses an anxiety that seems to be widely felt. This may be the real 'spectre of interdisciplinarity': the potential threat that the inherent, inclusive tendency of dance poses to the very existence of what others have called a 'marginal' and 'constitutionally fragile' discipline.[7]

Sometimes it seems as if *the discipline of dance itself* is the phantom, as definitions slip through our fingers like words falling away in the presence of dance. For André Lepecki, twentieth-century dance is defined by its association with movement, but for me, movement must always imply stasis, or inactivity, which is central to the compositional strategies of someone as 'purely' choreographic as Merce Cunningham. Movement is also the ground upon which another major art form is built: cinema. I prefer to turn to the mind/body relationship, the ground upon which somatic dance practices are built, to discover what distinguishes dance as a discipline. It is here that we find irreducible techniques, processes and knowledges that might constitute pure disciplinarity, but which also attract the attention of collaborators from other fields. So, beyond the politics and territorial manoeuvres that perhaps drive much of the disciplinary debate, we can work from two basic premises: one, that dance constitutes a unique field of knowledge grounded in somatic practices, and the other, that contemporary dance is increasingly the 'host' for the most progressive interdisciplinary practices. A brief survey of programming at major, progressive dance festivals in Europe will reveal much about the current state of the art of dance internationally, suggesting that while 'pure' dance works are few and far between, somatic practices underpin, and indeed allow for, the disciplinary, cultural and retrospective collaborations that are occurring.

Given our two basic premises, one of the questions we can ask is: what do the somatic and choreographic processes offer to interdisciplinary creative practitioners who continually return to the dancing body as their point of departure? In interviews conducted for this essay, I put this question to three Melbourne-based Australian choreographers, Gideon Obarzanek, Lucy Guerin and Helen Herbertson, who represent the public face of the art form locally through Obarzanek's state flagship company Chunky Move, the global profile of Australian dance through Guerin's international profile, and 'independent' dance through Herbertson's award-winning productions. All three negotiate distinct—but related—balancing acts between rigorous choreographic practices and integrated performance modalities. Obarzanek's body of work constantly prompts us to ask, 'Why dance?'; Guerin has engaged in intense collaborations with video artists, composers and designers that have supported her move away from the more formalist or minimalist focus of her early work; and Herbertson's most recent work with Ben Cobham has transformed the role of design in her dance performance. The co-existence of clear choreographic inquiry and interdisciplinary collaboration in the work of these choreographers provides fertile ground for the disciplinary issues I am concerned with here. The focus for all three on choreographic practice and process can perhaps be contrasted to the less clear-cut distinctions between *dance* and *performance* in the work of Sydney practitioners such as Martin Del Amo, Julie-Anne Long, Dean Walsh, Lee Wilson, Nikki Heywood and Tess De Quincey—all of whom move easily across both genres of programming. For some, this tendency in Sydney is the result of a lack of institutionalised dance at tertiary level in New South Wales, which has led to less distinct disciplinary formations being carried into the professional sphere. I shall return to this issue later.[8]

My question regarding the appeal and potential of dance in an interdisciplinary milieu seeks to invert power relations that typically work against dance, positioning it, not as responsive to, but generative of compositional strategies: ways of thinking about movement, gesture, time, rhythm, patterns and space, as well as expanding the potential of the body to produce meaning. This is certainly where Dance Studies is heading, as criticism moves away from a consideration of dance as reflective of, or responsive to, socio-cultural realities or concurrent aesthetic movements in other fields. Current writing argues for the notion of social choreographies in which dance plays a leading role in the micro and macro ecologies that shape our world.[9] Adaptability, openness, collaboration, inclusiveness—these are the terms that begin to define a discipline that is a far cry from the closed, inward-looking, exclusive profile so often implied by the term 'contemporary dance'.

The final section of this essay will consider the impact on dance training of new developments in the field of contemporary dance. How can the concept of 'technique' and associated systems of training be refigured to enable the collaboration, circulation and exchange that are apparent in the professional field?

1

Dance—a twentieth-century discipline?

'It is time, I believe, for dance scholars and researchers, especially those of us committed to the pursuit of practice-based research, to work towards a much more precise and nuanced articulation of the production of our difference.'

Elizabeth Dempster[10]

If the twentieth century was the period in which 'theatre dance beyond traditional forms' was established and defined in the West, it is there that we must first look in order to discover the essence of dance as a *discipline*, before coming to an understanding of its *interdisciplinarity*. For most of the last century, theatre dance was referred to as 'modern' dance, a term that fits nicely, and on various levels, with the idea that this was the era in which a discipline was defined. It was John Martin, dance critic for the *New York Times* from 1928 to 1962, who defined the term. By 1945, he had identified the key tenets of the new American dance in a series of lectures published as *The Modern Dance*. His description—of a stripped-back, essential yet experimental, approach to movement that explores interior states without reverting to mime or mimicry—helped set Western theatre dance on a linear progression through the rest of the century towards disciplinary purity.[11]

This progression entailed a gradual rejection of any non-essential elements and influences and a move towards an irreducible essence of the art form. Jumping in when things were getting particularly interesting in the mid-1940s, Merce Cunningham, a member of Martha Graham's company, was responding to a situation in which American modern dance had been established as a real alternative to classical ballet, but still depended heavily on other arts such as music and literature. Looking at these associated disciplines and the trajectory they were now following, Cunningham began to investigate the very conditions in which dance operated and which dictated its parameters, thus demonstrating his 'modernism'. 'For me,' he said, 'the subject of dance is dancing itself. It is not meant to represent something else, whether psychological, literary or aesthetic.'[12] Cunningham, in turn, was challenged by a new generation of dancers including his own, artists such as Steve Paxton, Lucinda Childs, Yvonne Rainer, Trisha Brown and Simone Forti. The resulting collective of avant-garde experimentalists, the Judson Dance Theatre (1962–64), significant figures in the period in Western theatre dance now referred to as 'postmodern', questioned just about anything that was left of the discipline. In fact, Rainer went on to write a manifesto that called for a rejection of spectacle, virtuosity, representation, empathy, style, voyeurism ... and even movement.[13] This group's activity, which was directly opposed to the types of dance practice that result in delineated techniques and set choreographies, seemed to directly challenge the idea of a *discipline of dance*. But in fact, this research made some headway toward a newly refined understanding of dance.

An important aspect of this influential New York-based development in theatre dance came from research undertaken elsewhere in American universities, which honed in on the mind/body processes that drive movement invention, as opposed to choreography based on existing dance techniques. A new attention to somatic experience, anatomical knowledge and kinaesthetic processes and awareness was being spearheaded by Anna Halprin, who had worked with Simone Forti between 1955 and 1959, with the aim of 'enrich[ing] our corporeal and kinetic imaginations directly—without recourse to external referents (literary or psychological) as had been the case up until then in most dance practices'.[14] Elizabeth Dempster would later describe the field of work that grew out of these origins as 'new movement practices', in which somatic techniques were taken up by choreographers and led to a clear 'linking of kinaesthesia and the imagination [...] towards physicalization of thought; insights about the body being expressed in transformed action'.[15] These included ideokinesis (to which Dempster is referring here) and the Alexander technique, but also 'various Eastern in-body disciplines' such as T'ai Chi Chuan, Aikido and Hatha Yoga.[16] These developments in Western theatre dance clearly connect with a history of exchange between choreographic practice and physical therapies that reaches from the influence of physical reforms in the nineteenth century down to the present.

These dovetailing developments in American universities, the New York artistic avant garde of the 1960s and the resulting revolution in American theatre dance, have now come to be referred to as 'postmodern' dance, a term that encompasses a variety of heterogeneous approaches to movement research. The somatic practices and choreographic developments emerging from this history have exerted a wide international influence and made a significant impact on Australian dance—see, for example, the work of Russell Dumas, Nanette Hassall, Rebecca Hilton, Phillip Adams, Lucy Guerin, Ros Warby—and been chronicled in our leading dance journal, *Writings on Dance*.

In this canonical model that crosses the twentieth century and beyond, dance—as a discrete discipline independent of the other art forms—has to be seen essentially as movement research resulting from mind/body processes, involving formal experimentation based on corporeal methodologies. While André Lepecki identifies movement as the key issue here, I prefer to believe that the exploration of *somatic intelligence* lies at the core of the discipline of dance. Somatic intelligence is a model of experience that places the body at the site where feelings or sensations are registered, feelings that may be untranslatable into language or any other medium, but which accumulate as corporeal knowledge. Even Lepecki believes that '[r]ethinking the subject in terms of the body is precisely the task of choreography'.[17] This is true of the most progressive forms of theatre dance operating today, whether or not they link directly to this postmodern lineage.

> Without making specific reference to somatic systems, Australian dance artist Rosalind Crisp, currently based at the Atelier de Paris-Carolyn Carlson, writes clearly about the mind/body work that informs her contemporary dance practice:

Dancing involves decision-making. The decision-making by the dancer interests me: the choreographic principles that guide the way she produces movement, the compositional causality of the movements, where they are initiated from in the body, with what speed or effort they are produced, at what level, in what direction, for what duration ... when.[18]

Crisp is describing the fundamental elements of physical movement—initiation, force, effort, time and space—and she goes on to elaborate the ways in which thought drives her experimentation with these elements: 'delaying or enlarging the beginnings of movements [...], alternating unpredictably between "going" and "not going"'.[19] An exploration of *decision-making in dance, the mind/body nexus that produces movement* independent of any 'foreign' elements or processes, has become the substance of Crisp's work (along with that of many others including American Deborah Hay) and it would seem to bring us very close to a definition of disciplinary purity. Yet at the same time it slips away. As Hay observed during one of her workshops: 'From the outside it is impossible to determine that discipline is being advanced', and argues that she prefers to 'democratize the tangible and intangible dynamics of discipline. There is no way discipline looks.'[20] The internal focus of mind/body approaches to dance and their resistance to traditional notions of technique, form and style, test our understanding of discipline, professionalism and processes of evaluation, performance and spectatorship. Yet disciplined this work certainly is.

If somatic intelligence explains how the dancer can occupy the very place where bodily knowledge demands attention but where discourse fails, we are perhaps getting close to explaining the value of such knowledge to experimental performance, performance that opposes language-based models of theatre and which, I believe, is intimately connected to dance as interdisciplinary practice. But it also explains the fragility of a discipline that operates outside or beyond normative codes and structures of knowledge. What needs protection, it would seem, is the validity of somatic research in and of itself. And since this 'heart' of the discipline is alive and kicking in both pure research and, as we shall see presently, *as a powerful force within interdisciplinary practice*, Elizabeth Dempster's call to arms in support of this work within the academy echoes further afield in the broader dance community, where protection may take a variety of forms: in Sydney, for example, the fight for studio space, which is so vital to the art form.

So perhaps my assertion that the discipline of dance is a twentieth-century phenomenon is less provocative than I suggested, if we take somatic intelligence to be at its heart. And the opposition between discipline and interdisciplinarity may have become less confrontational, if we think about how these knowledges operate in the work of Crisp, Warby and Guerin, artists who work intensively with text, projection and design respectively. Finally, it is somatic intelligence and all the associated somatic practices discussed here, both contemporary and historical, that provide the keys to a definition of the disciplinary distinctiveness of dance, and allow us to proceed to an enquiry into the position of dance's 'authority' in innovative, interdisciplinary performance practices.

2

Interdisciplinary continuity

'It is interesting that dance is so subject to concern about "discipline" when the non-conformism of other kinds of artists rarely raise the same anxieties.'

Sally Gardner[21]

The linear progression towards disciplinary purity does not tell the whole story of twentieth century dance. Alongside, and often overlapping with, this historical trajectory, another lineage of Western theatre dance sees choreography as a major force in the performance event, but only one element in a complex interdisciplinary dialogue with other artistic practices, sharing the *mise en scène* with set designs often by visual artists, original scores and/or live musicians, new technologies, and other modes of performance such as text-based theatre, pantomime, acrobatics and puppetry.

In light of this, we might view the canonical history just described through different lenses and see a very different picture. If Cunningham marked an historical point of 'modernist' disciplinary purity, he also picked up on disciplinary collaboration where others, such as the Ballets Russes before him, had left off. Cunningham built his aesthetic on the experimental composition theories of musician John Cage, and engaged American avant-garde visual artists Robert Rauschenberg and Jasper Johns as set-designers. Cunningham's collaborations with filmmakers such as Charles Atlas and Nam June Paik and the designers of virtual movement software, raised the bar set by Loïe Fuller at the turn of the century regarding creative partnerships between choreography and new technologies.[22]

Again the American postmodernists deserve special attention in any history of dance as interdisciplinary practice. Following Cunningham's lead, Judson Dance Theatre engaged in a productive exchange with developments in experimental music, art and performance in the New York avant garde of the 1960s. According to Simone Forti, '[a]t that time there weren't any firm boundaries between different artistic practices. We were all more or less concerned with an art of process.'[23] Originally married to visual artist Robert

Morris, Forti subsequently married experimental theatre-maker Robert Whitman and collaborated with him on his happenings. Yvonne Rainer, who was a key player in the early 1960s, exemplifies the disciplinary/interdisciplinary tensions of the period perfectly. Her contributions to reinventing the dancing body at this time were significant. By questioning assumptions about the kinds of dancing that supported contemporary systems of training, production and performance, Rainer and her colleagues continued the modernist interrogation of the disciplinary foundations of dance that had been carried out throughout the previous the twentieth century. However, she was working in a deeply interdisciplinary artistic milieu and Carrie Lambert-Beatty's recent monograph on her work in the 1960s recuperates Rainer as an artist who pre-empted, and possibly informed, philosophies and creative practices emerging around the same time as her choreographic research and performance.[24] Rainer's focus on issues of spectatorship—employing strategies such as averting her gaze while dancing and 'de-theatricalizing' the body—picked up on a major pre-occupation across the arts that would also inform her later filmmaking practice. What is most interesting here is the temporal concurrence of the most 'pure' manifestations of the moving body, and the most radical re-investments in interdisciplinarity in the work of Cunningham and the American postmodernists.

Enough about where we have been: where are we now, in Australia, and where are we going? 'Contemporary dance' is the term that has now replaced 'modern' and 'postmodern' dance, and which encompasses a very diverse body of current practices, including those that are tied genealogically to modernism and postmodernism in dance. French dance theorist Frédéric Pouillaude argues that a form such as contemporary dance does not represent 'the spirit of the time, the figure of the epoch', but something more akin to 'contemporaneity' as 'a *neutral simultaneity*, a *contingent coexistence* [...] all that belongs to a particular time'.[25] This definition can be applied to 'the contemporaneity of performers and onlookers', but also to the performance itself, which 'conserves the heterogeneity of the spectacular elements without heirarchizing them'.[26] Pouillaude believes this ability to maintain a 'neutral simultaneity' of the elements of a work to be specific to dance, distinguishing it from opera or theatre, where one field—the music or the script—tends to dominate the overall production, and he traces this heterogeneous approach to staging choreographic work back to the Ballets Russes. While one could argue that his definitions of opera and theatre are dated and that interdisciplinarity is an important part of these disciplines as they exist in contemporary culture, let's follow Pouillaude here as he argues that the tendency in dance is pronounced, endemic and historical.

Accepting the idea that contemporary dance is characterised by 'a *contingent coexistence*' of elements that *includes* choreography and dancing brings us to the important question of the position of dance within this 'heterogeneous' and 'non-heirarchialized' performance event. First, is Pouillaude's claim for contemporary dance in the twenty-first century reflected in the programming of key European dance festivals? While a fleeting survey cannot detail the status of the various disciplines included in a work, it can indicate how widespread the occurrence of interdisciplinary practice is in contemporary dance. We need only look at a handful of festivals held in 2010: the Festival Uzès Danse and Montpellier Danse in France; Julidans in Amsterdam, Tanz im August in Berlin and the Kunstenfestivaldesarts in Brussels.[27] If I am obliged to look overseas, it is because we have no international dance festivals in Australia. Furthermore, it is useful to place local work in a global context.

One interesting strand in the overall programming of these festivals turns to past work for inspiration, and the list of artists cited is telling. Taking the 2005 book Merce Cunningham, *Fifty Years* as his starting point, Boris Charmatz constructs a performance from its images and creates a live flip-book. Olga De Soto bases a 'performative lecture' on a 1932 piece by Kurt Joos in order to question 'the (im)possibility of reproducing dance pieces'. And Eszter Salamon adapts John Cage's 1949 'Letter on Nothing' to create *Dance for Nothing*. In a related vein, French-born dancer-choreographer Xavier Le Roy tries his hand at another genre, Butoh, but at a remove: employing a performance mode favoured by several other artists, he presents a lecture-demonstration of his work *Xavier makes some Rebutoh*, a trend that sees dancers sometimes doing more talking than dancing in their performances.

Le Roy, who worked as a guest artist with Chunky Move last year, is often included among contemporary dance practitioners whose work has been labelled 'conceptual dance'. Like that of Jérôme Bel, another French experimental artist interested in breaking down the barrier between artist and audience, and whose work also features in the festival programming, Le Roy's performances are highly self-reflexive and seek to test the very limits of the form. Lucy Guerin describes this work as she has experienced it:

> When you're talking about interdisciplinary ... well, it's interesting in Europe with the whole conceptual dance movement, where dance has pretty much dropped out of dance. I'm sure it's going to come back and it *is* coming back, but [there is this work] where you will just get people on stage talking about dance.

Such work has attracted considerable attention from dance theory, possibly due in part to its links, both explicit and implicit, with contemporary philosophy, but also to the controversial way it challenges *movement* as a defining characteristic of dance. This is made clear in the ambiguous title of André Lepecki's book on such artists, *Exhausting Dance*, and perhaps represents a kind of extreme within the field that is both refreshing and alarming, depending on your perspective.

In contrast to this, at the more mainstream Montpellier Festival there is still plenty of dancing from established artists such as Merce Cunningham, Régine Chopinot, Ohad Naharin, Anna Teresa De Keersmaeker and Jiri Kylian. William Forsythe, however, is represented by a series of videos and installations; Chopinot has a retrospective of his dance video work and Mathilde Monnier collaborates with a painter. The kind of integration of art forms and interrogation of 'performance' pioneered by artists like Stuart and Platel (both well represented in the programming) seems to be well established amongst the newer artists, many of whom have worked with them. There is a strong strand of work exploring variations on the traditional, stage-bound *mise en scène*, mostly through multimedia installation. Some, such as that of newcomers Pieter Ampe and Guilherme Garrido, start out as live performances, while others only exist as installations: Philip Gehmacher's *Dead Reckoning* and Zimmerfrei's *LKN Confidential*. Gehmacher also presents another work with Meg Stuart that lies somewhere between performance and installation. And there are explorations with other forms including the dance-drawing of Mono B. Conflating many of the major trends, ex-Stuart dancer Simone Aughterlony partners photographer and filmmaker Jorge León to present a film, performance and installation adapted from León's film about Indonesian migrants working as maids.

Many of the 'pure dance' works derive their cho-reographic content from traditional and folk-dance forms, including productions by Boyzie Cekwana and Lia Rodrigues, which draw on the movement language of their homelands, South Africa and Brazil respec-tively. This constitutes a strong overall trend, and so, an expansion of the art form to include non-Western colloquial and classical forms that trespass on the 'exclusive' traditional territory of the theatre dance canon. At the Uzès festival, usually the showcase for the new generation of artists, there is a return to pure dance, a reality that sets its face firmly against all my best attempts at grand and generalising provocations. Cecilia Bengolea and François Chaignaud present a work based on the Free Dance of François Malkovsky (1922–48) and elsewhere choreographers undertake compositional tasks such as reducing group choreographies to solos (Marc Vincent), or finding a gestural language that corresponds with the visual language of the war memorial (Laurent Pichaud). Exchanges with poetry and percussion, confined spaces and cinematographic techniques stay closely tied to the dancing body. What is absent are group works set in choreographed form. Perhaps what we can see in the younger generation's determined move away from set choreographies and return to improvisation-based performances is a departure from the 'discipline' of dance in its most traditional sense: that is, as structured choreographies using recognisable dance techniques by a professional and authoritative company leader. So, while interdisciplinarity is central to current practice, a question mark still hovers over the future. What a rapid survey *can* demonstrate is that there is no longer any disciplinary/interdisciplinary divide in contemporary dance; that both can exist across a single artist's body of work, and also co-exist within individual productions.

I want now to turn to the Australian scene, where interdisciplinarity also thrives, in order to look closely at the terms of its operations. How does the 'spectral', resistant and seemingly fragile discipline of dance take command of the interdisciplinary works presented as 'dance'? How is corporeally-based knowledge 'exported' into interdisciplinary performance, where it provides the ground upon which a work is built, rather than becoming a 'tool' for other disciplines? Do the other disciplines effectively accede or bend to the operations of dance? Can we identify compositional processes grounded in the somatic that are applied to other fields? And what does interdisciplinarity reveal about the discipline of dance?

Above all, what is it about dance that remains important for makers of interdisciplinary performance?

3

Interdisciplinary dance in Australia

'I wonder whether dance is kind of looking again [...] whether it's looking for its next phase.'

Helen Herbertson

At a dance conference in Melbourne in 2005, Australian dance critics and theorists Hilary Crampton, Maggi Phillips and Elizabeth Dempster drew attention to the status of the artistic discipline of dance, focusing mainly on the matter of sustainability. To counter what she called an 'alienating elitism', Phillips argued for an inclusivity that supported 'interconnections between the ecology of human behaviour and that of dance as an art-form'.[28] Similarly, Crampton argued for an 'expansion' of the dance field in the name of 'autonomy'—'I want to knock down the fences of the field to create a borderless place'—and cited as exemplary Chunky Move's pursuit of 'finding ways to engage audiences'.[29] More recently Sue Street has written on the topic, advocating 'participation' as the key to sustainability.[30] I, too, am concerned with the current state of the art, but my focus is not so much the sustainability of a form (whether through increasing audience numbers, or a limitless expansion of the field beyond those who identify as dance artists), as the profile of a discipline as it exists in current artistic practice within an increasingly interdisciplinary milieu. My interest here, I hope, is less *reactive* and more *responsive* to the directions artists are choosing for themselves. In my search for indications of the future direction of the art form, I shall turn now to the work of some of these artists.

While there has been much discussion about interdisciplinarity in dance theory, it is ironic—and surprising—that there has been so little about the creative operations of interdisciplinary practice. It is, after all, the developments in practice that have prompted the theory. For example, Susanne Franco and Marina Nordera argue that it was the critical theory revolution that shifted dance theory toward interdisciplinary methodologies:

> [P]redominantly aesthetic, historical, philological
> [...] analyses that characterized much prior research
> have given way to studies privileging the ways in
> which dance works as an art/or a social practice, its
> ideological charge, and its theoretical assumptions.
> [...T]his was accompanied by a general crisis in
> traditional disciplinary areas, a contamination of
> methodological tools, and the questioning of the
> artist's and the scholar's subjectivity.[31]

Clearly, a crisis in discipline, methodology, ideology and subjectivity—together with issues around dance as simultaneously a creative and social practice—began in choreographic composition and forced the shift in theory and criticism. The engagement of dance artists with contemporary theory has also been a key component in the developments in the art form that have challenged disciplinary boundaries, as the work of conceptual choreographers Jérôme Bel and Xavier Le Roy has shown.

I want to look closely here at the performance work of Gideon Obarzanek, Lucy Guerin and Helen Herbertson, all of whom successfully negotiate a path between an overtly interdisciplinary approach to the *mise en scène* and a commitment to choreographic research and crafting. And here we touch on another nexus in contemporary dance: between 'perform- ance' and 'practice'. The disciplinary characteristic of somatic intelligence identified earlier does not necessarily assume 'performance', but is invariably associated with rigorous *research through practice*. Yet the interdisciplinary tendency in dance has been consistently associated in this essay with performance outcomes. Again here I am following Pouillaude, who insists that it is only through performance that 'dance can constitute and offer itself as an *oeuvre* [a work]'.[32] In terms of my central argument regarding inter/ disciplinarity, the condition of dance in the twenty- first century needs to be understood through public art practice, the profile of which shapes the general understanding of the field in the wider community.

What Obarzanek, Guerin and Herbertson have in common is an investment in rethinking the *mise en scène* of contemporary dance, which, in Pouillaude's definition, 'conserves the heterogeneity of the spectacular elements [he means, potentially, light, props, sets, sculptures, bodies, reproduced images, costumes, motion-sensor technology, animals etc] without hierarchizing them'. The temptation here is to claim for dance a model in which choreography becomes the dominating force that calls all the other elements of the *mise en scène* into its 'order.' Because surely, in the case of 'unhierarchized' heterogeneity, dance would risk losing any sense of aesthetic centrality or 'ownership'. It is these issues that I discussed with the three local artists.

Given their intense collaborations in other disciplines, I began by asking why they keep returning to dance. For both Obarzanek and Guerin this question is their starting-point. Interrogating the role of dance in our broader lives is a constant, underlying enquiry that not only drives Obarzanek's search for relevance, but also raises the issue for his audiences: '[H]aving to do that for myself every time [I make a work ...] does it for the ones who watch it too.' He confesses, oddly perhaps, that he has 'never been a huge fan of dance'—

> It's not that I don't like dance, I do like it and I choose to work in it, but ... I often question it. I don't know whether it's that interesting. I don't know whether it merits being on its own. I know how incredibly fragile and difficult it is to build some kind of sense of something ... and how easily it's punctured and disappears. [...] So a lot of my works are a question about dance itself through other things.[...] In every show [...] I have to prove to myself that dance is worthwhile.

27

Whether surveying Australian audiences about what they would like to see in a dance performance (*Wanted – Ballet for a Contemporary Democracy*, 2002), asking middle-aged men when and why they dance (*I Want to Dance Better at Parties*, 2004), or making a new media work that takes light and movement as its point of departure (*Glow*, 2006), his choreographies often view dance from a perspective beyond the obvious formal and aesthetic concerns generally associated with contemporary dance.

Guerin, too, asks fundamental questions of the discipline, and like Obarzanek, she often begins 'somewhere else'. However, rather than testing dance from new perspectives, she enjoys the challenge of phenomena that are not immediately suggestive of movement. Sleep, the details of a particular crime, the tone of endings, a construction disaster and our experience of information networks have all been some of her starting-points:

> I really seek to show that dance has its own form of communication and to try to understand what that is and what is powerful about it. [...I want to] find how dance speaks about our world, rather than just always about my internal state, because I think that is a much more natural role for dance but also one that's been explored a lot. [...] I think we're in a time now where people really want to look beyond their own internal turmoil and really do want to connect, want to get ideas from the community and the world.

While Guerin is clearly comfortable in her role as a chore-ographer, Obarzanek enjoys moving between jobs—from visual artist-designer, to working with sound and even acting as stage director of some of his works. But when pressed on why, in spite of himself, he keeps returning to dance, he talks of its capacity for abstraction, the oscillation between corporeal familiarity and alienation, and the power of movement within the staging of the creative event—themes that dance has evoked strongly and frequently for centuries.

Obarzanek describes a process of abstraction, particularly in stylised forms of dance, whereby the dancer can 'transcend themselves being [a particular] identity to becoming almost identity-less and they become part of movement, they become part of life, they become part of music, they become—it's like dance itself'. This echoes some of the earliest writing on twentieth-century theatre dance by the French Symbolists who were inspired by the Romantic bal-let, the extraordinary Löie Fuller and others. They understood dance as an activity of transformation and fluidity that defies definition, and this became a model for their new poetics that tested the limits of language. Elsewhere I have argued that dance often functions as an 'oppositional' force, due to its ability to operate as an alternative to language. For this reason contemporary dance continues to be associated with the artistic avant-garde and allows choreographers like Obarzanek to engage in experimental approaches while keeping an eye on relevance.

Both Guerin and Obarzanek play with the ten-sions between the spectacular, but also specialised, movements of dance, and everyday movements with which an audience is instantly able to connect, and which point, as Helen Herbertson puts it, to the fact that 'you're watching a human'. Obarzanek describes the former as 'extended' movements that go 'into kinetics that are just not done', with the latter being connected to muscle memory, gestural habits and their stylisation. In her most recent work, *Human Interest Story* (2010), Guerin is 'interested [...] to see if the movement can be pushed outwards to connect with more day-to-day, real-life events'.[33] And from this work she gave me a specific example:

> [I]t's almost like they're dropping in and out of the performance, because some of the movement is high-ly contrived and highly stylised and choreographed and then everything will freeze and [a dancer] will just walk out of the picture and do her hair.

Perhaps it is because of our intimacy with the central medium of the art form, the body, that this shift between the familiar and the unfamiliar through physical movement is such a powerful tool for dance. Much has been written about a physical form of empathy that is triggered in dance performances: the theory argues that dance is effective as a mode of performance because of universal corporeal experiences such as the effect of gravity or the sensation of falling, which are activated and manipulated through choreography. Accordingly, thanks to this fundamental corporeal connection, the spectator is able to follow the body away from the familiar and toward abstraction, or vice versa.

On the subject of stylised movement, Guerin also talks about a shift away from more shape- and line-based movement and towards less formally determined compositional starting-points. Her work is characterised by a fine choreographic craftsmanship—Mikhail Baryshnikov, for whom she has choreographed, noted her ability to do a lot with a limited set of movements—so this shift away from more formal concerns is noteworthy:

I've become more interested in almost tonal movement or the textures of movement or the different
sort of tensions or dynamics that can exist in the
body, and letting that define the shape. So it might
be about shaking or it might be about straight spiky
lines ... but that kind of idea then creates movement, rather than going, 'Okay, put your arm there
and put your leg there.'

As a starting-point for movement generation, these tones,
textures, tensions and dynamics do come from the moving
body itself, but they are also in and of themselves non-
discipline-specific, so are able to be moved or translated
from choreographic processes across to other disciplines. In
fact, Herbertson begins with writing, a compositional process that offers key terms which she describes in similarly
generic ways: texture, colour, density, rhythm, action. In
her process, they move from the page into her movement
research, where they combine with other influences and
continue to develop into a 'really solid physicality'. The
words fall away, for the most part, and this new physical
manifestation enters into dialogue with her collaborators.

So, in a work that transfers compositional ideas
from the moving body to other art forms, movement
can become a powerful point of departure that allows
those ideas to circulate and influences the entire *mise en
scène*. But the important role of movement, rather than
bringing closure, also facilitates an open and expanded
kind of dialogue with its audience, putting the viewer
into circulation as well. Obarzanek describes a scene
from his *Mortal Engine*, devised in 2008, in which he
explores choreography, motion-sensor technologies
and graphic/lighting effects. *Mortal Engine* is a science
fiction-laced spectacle that moves from an intimate

opening solo, in which a single body activates pat-
terned light effects on a 'touch-screen' the size of the
stage, to a 'smoke and laser' dominated finale that
dwarfs the still bodies onstage and is reminiscent of
the dance parties of the 1990s. Here movement drives
the shift from narrative to abstraction:

> [Y]ou have a situation where two people are up
> against a wall and you recognise their relationship
> to each other, but then movement becomes its own
> thing and becomes sensory, so then eventually bod-
> ies almost disappear, and then literally disappear,
> and then it just becomes the rhythm of light and
> motion [...], as an audience [member], to experience
> a narrative then becomes like a sensory experience.
> It's not [merely] narrative any more.

In this scenario the moving body is somewhere to start,
but an integrated, sensorially charged *mise en scène* is the
finishing-point.

Herbertson's investment in the leading role dance
can play regarding the transformation of the *mise
en scène* is clear in two recent works, *Morphia Series*
(2002) and *Sunstruck* (2008). Both employ relatively
low-tech elements to focus and guide the audience's
experience. The set for *Morphia Series*, a solo work
designed for an audience of twelve, is a box that
contains Herbertson in a shape of the dancer's dimen-
sions. The tiny audience are accommodated on mobile
seating that rolls them up close to the dancer from
far away. Also, in a radical design, the performance
evolves in a low spectrum of light that challenges the
spectator's perception. *Sunstruck*, on the other hand,
is designed for venues with open, vast interiors, and
uses a circular seating arrangement to create an inti-

mate, impermanent, performance space for its two male dancers, Trevor Patrick and Nick Sommerville. As it circles on its dolly and track behind the ring of audience chairs, a large spotlight makes a train-like clacking sound, and throws light on the unfolding duet in a seemingly random way. While she may begin with language, Herbertson's performance events are careful productions of an 'open', sensory experience that is truly irreducible:

> We're working incredibly hard to land the audience in the right kind of place to be open to this openness ... so they're able to have [access to] what's there. Because it is always strange; I know it's strange and it's not a story and there's not a huge amount to hang on to, but if you can come to it, then you can really get a lot out of it. You can dream sideways with it, you can understand it ... *Sunstruck*, fathers, sons, the land, seasonal, cycles, life, death again. [...I]t's experiencing a sense of being alive or something, something big, big—but open.

That the moving body can often leave little to 'hang on to' seems to be the strength of this kind of work: a performance event that is based on the deep complexity of the moving bodies in the central duet, but expands to say something about human relationships and about life more generally.

When it comes to translating choreographically-based knowledges and processes across to other elements of the *mise en scène*, the traditional proce-dure—whereby a choreographer devises material, teaches it to her dancers, then invites in collaborators, be they composers or lighting designers, to complete the work—is jettisoned. Herbertson describes this kind of contemporary dance as 'new work', meaning that nothing precedes the creative process. For her, 'dance is always in that open grid where anything is possible', allowing for 'lots of play and input' with and by collaborators. The starting-point of most choreographic work is a 'blank canvas', an 'open' position. This ensures two things: that the emerging somatic research and experimentation are the driving forces of the work, and that there is room for exchange with other contributors. And these two things go hand-in-hand. Both somatic processes and experimentation require an artist to be open and ready to respond in the moment, maintaining a position where decision-making is foregrounded and interrogated, down to the line of the gaze and the curve of the spine. It is into this environment that collaborators are invited, one in which options may remain open right up until the moment of the performance event itself.

For Guerin, the collaborative process starts with the dancers: 'I bring something pretty loose into the studio because I feel [that] certain things come out of the physical practice [and it is these] that really shape the concept.' An important point here is the expectation of many choreographers that their dancers take part in the research and experimentation phase. This was the subject of Amanda Card's *Body for Hire?: The State of Dance in Australia*.[34] The involvement of dancers in the choreographic process seemed so pervasive in contemporary Australian dance in 2006 that Card proposed a radical change to company structures so as to create a 'dancer-driven' model, placing the dancers in more stable employment and inviting choreographers to work with them on a project-by-project basis. The collaborative demands placed on dancers are certainly something that needs to be addressed in their training programs, and I shall return to the issue later.

Obarzanek's first explorations with new media technologies for the stage, the solo work *Glow*, began with a foundational collaboration with Frieder Weiss, a German interactive systems design engineer. The creative development that ensued was one in which the dancing body was not necessarily the central concern. However, what began as an experiment with light and movement (the same 'touch-screen' effect employed in *Mortal Engine*) somehow resulted in a concise and complete dance work about the body and technology. In *Glow*, the female dancer's movements are limited to the ground as she activates the motion sensor technology, generating the abstract white effects and patterns that surround her on the screen surface on which she is dancing. Drama is introduced into the limited performance space—on which the audience look down from above on all sides—in the form of black shadows which engage with the dancer in increasingly menacing ways.

Obarzanek is very clear about who it is that leads his creative process:

> I work very much *with* my collaborators. I generate a lot of the material first, and a lot of my composers that I work with and [in the case of] Frieder...the other forms analyse that and start to build things around [it]. Other times it's the other things [that] are first or simultaneous […,] but it's not about choreography and dance *responding* to other art forms. It certainly doesn't feel like that in the studio. (*My emphasis*)

For Guerin, too, dance is central: 'I like the dance to be the defining art form.' Her ideal scenario is one in which collaborators are 'trying to realise my vision [...] through what they do' and she suggests that this relationship works best when her co-artists have a history of working with dance. In these cases, 'the movement comes first and then I do like it to be pushed around a bit by other disciplines'. Getting the balance between collaborators wrong, however, can lead to problems:

> I think I need to kind of protect [dance] or some-
> thing ... because I think music particularly, and
> lighting, can really dominate, can really become the
> leaders, especially music. [...] I always feel that to
> make a dance to a piece of music is cheating because
> the mood is already there, the emotion is there, the
> structure is there, [and] all you have to do is kind
> of slot into that. [However] it's very seductive and
> it's what we've done for centuries, really.

Guerin and Obarzanek share the impulse about 'standing ground', so that while the starting-point for a work may come from unlikely, external phenomena, a crucial aspect of the creative process is discovering precisely what it is that dance can bring to the task of production and how it can muster other artistic disciplines along the way.

One element of production that jumps off the stage in all three choreographers' work is set and lighting design. Indeed, in so far as it occupies 3-dimensional space—and time, too, in the case of moving parts and images—design has most in common with the fundamental elements of the moving body. One of Australia's most successful design partners for live performance is Bluebottle 3, founded by Ben Cobham and Andrew Livingstone in Melbourne in 1991. Cobham has worked with both Guerin and Herbertson, creating productions that are exemplary in respect of an integrated *mise en scène*. Guerin worked with the team on her 2006 production of *Structure and Sadness*, a work devised as a response to the Westgate Bridge collapse while it was under construction in Melbourne in 1970. The set design involved a human-scale 'house of cards' built by the dancers as the performance proceeded— literally between duets and group work— only to be collapsed in a domino effect half-way through. Planks of wood provide the third part of a trio and seesaws that literally illustrate cantilevering. The second half featured the designers themselves 'building' a replica of the Westgate Bridge against the stage backdrop by adjusting the strip neon lights that had been in place from the beginning of the show. Bluebottle 3 collaborates in a most distinctive way, as Guerin describes when explaining the creative process undertaken for *Structure and Sadness*:

> Working with Bluebottle, we would have workshop weeks where we would work with lights and it would be much more integrated. [...T]hey don't like to work separately... The building of that structure, I don't know what discipline you'd call [it], sculpture or building or engineering, [but] the whole dance happened around [it]. I did have a lot of the material before we had that idea, so then it was a question of how to bring those things together and make this durational thing happen. [...] I loved doing that piece because of the way the set and the movement were part of the same activity and one bled into the other.

Here, as choreography lends inspiration to the set design and the design in turn 'pushes' the choreography 'around', an intimate dialogue is created.

In the case of Herbertson's work with Cobham, the dialogue reaches a more intimate level. Having arrived at a physicality driven by her writing and other influences such as images, Herbertson enters into a formative dialogue with Cobham, whose contribution extends to lighting design. A period of experimentation would occur, she explains, with Cobham working 'inside what's beginning to take shape' as a 'set structure [with] 'light':

> Some of the morphing and adapting of the [movement] scores happens in response to what the light wants, so something might not really work in that three-dimensional way of working. [...T]he light and the set really play a bit of an editing and generating role at a time when the [movement] scores are [...] not fully formed.

The scores Herbertson is referring to form the basis of the structured improvisation that constitutes the choreographic component of the performance. The idea that the movement content can be responsive to 'what the light wants' suggests a magical synthesis of elements that are able to sustain their heterogeneity and at the same time create a space in which the audience's response may occur. The research interests she shares with Cobham—issues of scale, the nature of perception and means of creating imaginative space—all come into play here: 'You both come with something that you're interested in and see if they fit together.'

Ironically, in view of the traditional opposition of language and dance, it is words that often facilitate the process of interdisciplinarity in dance. Writing is an important part of Herbertson's process and performances, and can provide 'the triggers that set some improvisation score in motion or the energy trigger in a scene that will shift something sideways'. A generative mode of writing can also provide key compositional ideas relating to texture, colour and rhythm, all of which she can share with Cobham. But when the work finally reaches the public stage, Lucy Guerin's observation—that language is a 'sort of pointy expression', while dance 'can sort of synthesise things that we can't necessarily speak about so easily'—is played out in the few words that are ultimately heard in Herbertson's performances. In a reversal of traditional performance-making, *writing* is a creative tool that gives way, in the final production, to the contingent coexistence of the non-language based elements of the performance event.

We are left, it seems, in a situation in which tussles about leaders and followers fall away and the work of art just does its work. Yet, as we shall see, Herberston is also a fierce defender of the disciplinary distinctiveness of dance. Taken collectively, these three modes of contemporary dance practice describe a model in which textures, rhythms, actions and tensions realised through movement research enter into translations, movements and exchanges that in turn bring the audience into circulation with the heterogeneous elements of the work of art. What appears to matter most is how you bring your audience to where 'they're able to have [access to] what's there'. There's nothing specifically choreographic about that objective, only a world of difference in how you get there and what's on offer.

Based on the case studies discussed here, we could conclude that the discipline of dance is quietly, but confidently, assertive in Melbourne. This is apparent in Guerin and Obarzanek's conscious and self-reflexive testing of their medium with challenging subject matter,

complex performance events, and sophisticated collaborations. It is also apparent in the carefully crafted
choreographic sequences that move easily between the
technically spectacular and the everyday body. There
is really no question of dance being lost in the mix in
their work, but fascinating nuances in the masterful way
that the discipline calls its collaborators to work towards
choreographically determined goals. This disciplinary
clarity combined with collaborative experimentation
make Herbertson, Guerin and Obarzanek ideal repre-
sentatives for the form both here and internationally.

4

Training future dance artists

It is that capacity [of dance] to be specific, physically specific, that's the thing.
You can't do that without training, you
really can't.

Helen Herbertson

Dance training is a fraught topic. It needs to be
ongoing, but at the same time it's expensive.
Systems that 'indoctrinate' the body require
counter-systems that 'release'. Rigorous practice in
one system can limit 'versatility'. Physical ability can

exclude disability. Time spent in the lecture-theatre or the seminar-room is time away from the studio. Whether we need technicians or well-rounded artists is only the first of many issues that need to be addressed, and the limits of this essay preclude my dealing with all of them. I want, therefore, simply to consider various ways of understanding the 'discipline of dance' in relation to training, and the implications for dance programs if interdisciplinarity in dance in the twenty-first century is indeed as 'pronounced, endemic and historical' as Pouillaude has argued.

The technical systems associated with 'the trained dancer' were conspicuously absent from my account of the disciplinary specificity of dance in the first part of this essay, namely classical ballet and the modern idioms of which the Graham and Cunningham techniques are the most popular. When we think about dance and discipline, what is most likely to spring to mind is the image of the dancer sweating it out in the studio, wrestling with the potential and limitations of the body and striving toward a technical ideal. I have purposely avoided this image for several reasons, the main one being the dilemma around *what technique?* Does technique really matter? Is dance training something that belongs exclusively to the classroom, a way to keep in shape, a means to an end? Or is it fundamental, given the way in which somatic knowledge sets the parameters for the form? On a recent visit to Sydney, American choreographer Tere O'Connor spoke of his understanding that training systems and the creative practice of choreography are activities that do not necessarily line up in a one-to-one relationship. As he put it; you don't put scales into a musical composition.

Traditional dance techniques still play a major role in most international dance conservatoriums and tertiary-education programs, and a choreographer like Lucy Guerin would still expect this kind of technical proficiency from her dancers, even though she may ask them to leave certain expectations at the door:

> It's really tricky because these dancers come into the studio and they're highly trained and they're highly skilled. They can do all these amazing jumps and turns and steps and then I just want them to vibrate or I want them to do these [other] things. But it's funny, I really do need them to have had that training before they can do what I want them to do. It's quite interesting because sometimes I do want them to be able to refer to that [training] or pull that out.

Guerin is describing a co-existence here between training methods that produce dancers with a more-or-less definable set of skills, and collaborative choreographic processes that depend on the open-ended enquiry of somatic practices. While she is inviting her dancers into an experimental, improvisation-based situation, where the aim is to find the right movements *whatever they might be*, a background in and understanding of the codes, techniques and skills associated with established systems is essential background 'body knowledge'.

This is not to suggest that formal dance training systems do not deal in somatic knowledges, but rather to acknowledge a fundamental difference in the kind of *authority* at play: on the one hand, the ideal of the codified form is the aspiration, and, on the other, the aspiration is authored by the dancer. The first might be seen as corresponding to institutionalised systems of knowledge, the point Elizabeth Dempster seemed to be making in 2005, when she called for the protection of the disciplinary specificity of dance in the university context. Arguing that dance is an 'undisciplined discipline' that is unique, specialised and generative of 'unregulated' knowledges and processes, she presents a case-study of the somatic practice of ideokinesis, which, she contends, is an example of 'empirical, in-body research, whose vitality is contingent upon its ongoing resistence to professionalism and regulation'. (This 'resistance to regulation' is shared, to a greater or lesser degree, by many of the somatic practices outlined earlier.) She contrasts this to 'professionally' orientated models of the art of dance and the kinds of techniques they mobilize.[35] More recently Dempster has written:

> Dance technique has often been conceived as a means whereby personal, subjective aspects of embodiment are transmuted and put to work in service of a 'higher' artistic purpose. Thus the function of dance technique in a discipline such as ballet, for example, is both positive, that is producing quantifiable skills and abilities, and also negative—reducing elements of 'personality' or idiosyncratic behaviour which might detract from or otherwise present an obstacle to realisation of the choreographic idea.[36]

The technical dancer as a conduit or vehicle for someone else's choreographic vision is set in opposition here to *self-authoring* dance artists working in movement systems and methodologies that are resolutely unquantifiable. If dance techniques aimed at producing professionals can be aligned with institutionalisation—to which an 'undisciplined,' experimental approach is considered resistant—then I would suggest that, in this regard, dance in no way differs from any other creative practice in the academy.

In my own experience at the University of New South Wales, vocationally-based intentions sit very uneasily alongside research-based aspirations, both creative and theoretical. So perhaps we can talk about types of training, creative production and theory that correspond with 'systems of control', and other varieties that test the limits of language and discourse, for example, types of dance that correspond with 'professionalism' and types of theory that test the limits of language.

But if there is something *particularly* precarious about dance as creative practice in the university, perhaps we should be clear what we mean by *undisciplined* dance and technically *disciplined* dance, polar opposites in this field, in order to ask how both might operate side by side in the tertiary world. And what are the implications of this complexity for dancers who will very likely find themselves in the increasingly inter-disciplinary, collaborative condition of contemporary dance? On the one hand, disciplined dance looks like a closed system with a clear outcome, that of producing dancers to be put into the service of others, including those working in an interdisciplinary milieu. On the other hand, what Dempster refers to as 'undisciplined' dancing would seem to offer more potential for both empowering dance as a creative force/leader *and also* allowing for an outward, inclusive focus that rattles the dividing bars of disciplinary cages. Given the need for both models to be allocated dedicated studio time, the question is: how are 'dance artists in training' to be accommodated alongside those in other creative disciplines with whom they may potentially work?

But, if it's not stating 'the bleedin' obvious', we can't have interdisciplinarity without disciplinary specificity. I can't help thinking that, however unfashionable he might have become these days, Merce Cunningham was way ahead of us all. His ability to make dance speak about the (urban) human condition directly, without reference to anything exterior, and articulated exclusively through bodies moving in space and time, gave a firm disciplinary backbone to his interdisciplinary performance work. For Lucy Guerin, too, that same firm backbone of learned technique is vital, something against which to react, and she is desperate for it not to disappear:

> My big worry is that there won't be highly-trained dancers to then subvert [… T]hat's kind of how I've always worked. […I]t doesn't have to be Graham technique, it doesn't have to be ballet, it doesn't really matter what it is, but to really rigorously explore a physical practice to a highly, highly rigorous point is really, really, really important and I think with some of those [interdisciplinary] models, the students don't get that. Because it is more conceptual, it's more about integrating, but there's not necessarily anything to integrate. I mean you can see that some people do study ballet, some people study release techniques, some people study Cunningham or Graham—and all good things can come out of all of those [techniques], but I think the thing that is important is to have experienced a really intense and defined and articulate physical practice that

doesn't come from intellectualising, but is fully, fully, fully embodied and experienced and physical. That's what defines dance as opposed to, say, performance or some other physical [art] forms.

So, back to somatic, embodied knowledge and intensive physical training. Many of the artists cited in this essay are living proof that this is where it all begins. Guerin studied dance at the Centre for Performing Arts in Adelaide, Obarzanek at the Australian Ballet School and Herbertson was classically trained in Queensland. Of course, we shouldn't kid ourselves that institutionalised forms of education are an artist's only means of preparation. Individuals will find what they need where they can. But at the same time, surely new developments in dance pedagogy—for dancers, choreographers, theorists and arts workers—need to be responsive to the state of the art 'in the field'. And surely a dance program can accommodate both intensive training, and exposure to other relevant art forms and also the big ideas that bind them all together.

One program that seems to have managed just that is the Certificate of Training Cycle/Diploma offered by P.A.R.T.S. (Performing Arts Research and Training Studios), established in 1995 in association with the Rosas dance company in Brussels. As its name makes clear, P.A.R.T.S. is responsive to the needs of both the industry *and* research. Indeed, it was devised in consultation with progressive and successful artists who bridge the two, including Anne Teresa De Keersmaeker, director of Rosas. The foundations of the program are 'improvisation, composition, release technique, theatre and music'.[37] Recognized for its pedagogical innovation, P.A.R.T.S seems to be confronting the technique/research and discipline/interdisciplinary tensions very successfully, accommodating both the dancer and the choreographer, and the movement between these two positions. They also have strengths in history and theory. With a rigorous audition process and modest fees that cover the costs of a daily macrobiotic lunch, Nalina Wait describes this program as 'a contemporary dancer's dream [...], dreamt up by a deep-thinking contemporary dance artist and carefully crafted to create the ideal (and perhaps idealistic) scenario'.[38]

While the historical, cultural and financial circumstances that gave rise to P.A.R.T.S make such an organisation unimaginable in Australia, a confluence of major shifts is occurring in the disciplinary field right here in New South Wales, including the increasing interdisciplinarity that has been the subject of this essay, more clearly focused understandings of the practice/research nexus, the ongoing, rumbling crisis for the New South Wales dance community, and shifts in the sparse tertiary landscape for dance in New South Wales. In respect of the depths to which interdisciplinary practice runs, the New South Wales dance scene, concentrated in Sydney, differs significantly from that in Victoria and other states, and perhaps this means that a strictly disciplinary approach to the pedagogy in Sydney is ill-suited to the local environment.

Let me turn for a moment to this distinction between the kind of interdisciplinarity that is occurring in Sydney and that which flourishes in Melbourne. While we can identify a disciplinary assertiveness in the work of Guerin and Obarzanek in particular, something different is going on in Sydney, and Herbertson's description of the 'open grid' of contemporary dance will help us understand what it is. While somatic knowledge determines the 'open' quality of her productions, a real equity is apparent between the elements of the work which appear impossible to unravel or return to some kind of discrete condition. This could also be said of the work of many NSW-based artists, some of whom I have already mentioned. Soloist Martin del Amo works with autobiographical spoken text and improvised live music by Gail Priest. Julie-Anne Long also uses spoken word in her solo work and has had many artistic collaborators from various fields, most recently video artists Samuel James and Kate Murphy and photographer Heidrun Löhr. Force Majeure is one of Australia's leading dance theatre companies, employing a clever mix of actors and dancers, and director Kate Champion has long-standing creative partners in designer Geoff Cobham and video artist Brigid Kitchin. Lee Wilson and Mirabelle Wouters' Branch Nebula creates unique dance theatre work fuelled by an interest in 'kickboxing, wrestling, speed-way, video arcades, BMX competitions, art exhibitions, peep shows or just doing our shopping at the local mall'.[39] Nikki Heywood describes herself as 'an independent multi-disciplined artist with a background in movement-based theatre', and engages with text in diverse and experimental ways. And Tess de Quincey's company has explored partnerships with musicians, video artists, poets and actors. But this pattern also applies to the more 'choreographic' artists such as Sue Healey and Narelle Benjamin, who multi-task across dance and film, creating performances that include projection, installation works, and short films. To lay oneself open to the potentially dominating elements that Guerin referred to requires what I can only call a disciplinary humility on the part of Herbertson and many of these Sydney-based artists. This provides the ideal conditions for collaborative experimentation due to a softening of that assertion, a softening that seems in keeping with the essence of dance as movement and fluidity, but also in line with the nature of somatic knowledge as an open, unregulated process.

Along with this widespread interdisciplinarity, the explicitly technical kind of dancing is less apparent in Sydney than in the South, except in the work of the flagship Sydney Dance Company which does seem to 'hover above us'. This raises particularly interesting questions in regard to traditional ideas about discipline and pedagogical considerations. The situation in Sydney has perhaps been brought about by a lack of continuity in dance performance degrees in New South Wales: the dance program at the University of Western Sydney was closed down several years ago; Macquarie University recently initiated dance courses, but no complete program; and the University of New South Wales offers a Dance Education degree with no performance major. This means that the reiteration of disciplinary standards is not as apparent as in Perth, Adelaide, Brisbane or Melbourne, where dance performance programs are well established at local universities. Added to this is the fact that many of our dance artists have been trained interstate, thus leaving their 'disciplined' days far behind them, leaving them open to a greater diversity of influences. One important result of the condition of tertiary dance in New South Wales was the 'independent' tutelage provided by Rosalind Crisp at Omeo Studios in Sydney in the 1990s, which encouraged young dancers to experiment with a unique, rigorous but 'undisciplined' kind of movement research that was fiercely independent of any established systems.

This has all produced an environment in which interdisciplinarity has flourished. Another important historical factor is the influence on the local scene of the Performance Space, which has provided a focus for experimental performance across disciplinary divides in this city for the past three decades. Dance has always played an important role in the programming at this Sydney institution. Part of the softening of a disciplinary hardline in Sydney may also be linked to an increase in research and development, fostering interdisciplinarity through experimentation. Opportunities for creative development in Sydney have dramatically increased, thanks to the establishment in 2004 of Critical Path Choreographic Laboratory, which provides practical 'support for experienced choreographers to tailor make research projects addressing their personal needs'.[40] While this has been beneficial, it has not been matched by an increase in performance opportunities, with the result that developments and showings far outnumber opening nights, and artist-run performance events are the main means of circulating work. This raises the issue of 'process' versus 'performance' again: an increasing emphasis on the former challenges ideas about 'production' and 'dissemination' that are associated with establishing 'disciplinarity'. These differences between Melbourne and Sydney, and between assertive disciplinarity and intense interdisciplinarity, suggests that there is a need in Sydney for training programs and other supporting resources—such as open classes and networking opportunities—that respond to the conditions 'in the field' in a forward-looking and, perhaps, experimental way.

Let me conclude with some serious questions. How can we create for our dance artists in New South Wales an environment that reflects the conditions defining the current field, that recognises the strengths of the local scene but lends stronger support to its growth and development? How can we begin to generate that new and 'emerging' wave of dance artists that are so notably absent from the current contemporary dance environment in Sydney? A better understanding of the operations of interdisciplinarity in dance is, I believe, a good place to start. This essay has only just begun to explore in detail the compositional labour of interdisciplinarity in contemporary dance, and what this labour might reveal in favour of *the choreographic* as a body of knowledge that exceeds its disciplinary parameters through openness, collaboration, self-reflexivity and yes, movement. One of its aims has been to consider dance as a generator of compositional strategies—ways of thinking about rhythm, dynamics, patterns, tone, space and time—in order to lay to rest for good the idea of dance being colour and movement within a larger whole that is focused elsewhere (on story, music etc.) Another has been to think through exactly how the very nature of dance, as experimental, inclusive and non-linear, facilitates collaborative work. These are the choreographic knowledges and processes offered by dance in the creative development stage to which other disciplines keep returning. I believe dance itself provides the 'ground' upon which the kinds of collaborations that truly test disciplinary boundaries rest. Perhaps, with a better understanding of the labour of interdisciplinary creativity, we can get closer to understanding the true state of a discipline that ultimately, despite my best efforts here, remains 'spectral'.

I shall give the last word to Sydney independent choreographer, dancer and curator, Emma Saunders, who sums up our progress, fears, hopes and wishes:

> There's more to dance than technique and training. We know that now ... but lights flicker on and off and give hope to what some call a dead art form. Oh no, I say, I say. Don't go out so easy—this form is alive and high kicking in all its glory, just a little more crooked, unsettled, less obvious and continually questioned (we hope).[41]

Endnotes

1   'A View from the Outside / A View from the Inside', in
    What I Think about When I Think about Dancing, exhibi-
    tion catalogue, ed. by Lisa Havilah, Emma Saunders
    and Susan Gibb (Campbelltown: Campbelltown Arts
    Centre, 2009), p.99.
2   'Editorial', *October* 10 (1979), p.3.
3   See Erin Manning, *Relationscapes: Movement, Art,
    Philosophy* (Cambridge, Mass.: MIT Press, 2009); André
    Lepecki, *Exhausting Dance* (New York: Routledge, 2006)
    and Philipa Rothfield 'Differentiating Phenomenology
    and Dance', *Topoi* 24 [2005], pp.43-53, for the reso-
    nance of diverse dance practices with contemporary
    philosophical concerns such as the 'movement of
    thought', 'intensity' and 'the interval' (Manning),
    'presence,' 'subjectivity,' and the 'body without organs,'
    (Lepecki) 'becomings,' 'perception,' and 'embodiment'
    (Rothfield).
4   J.T Klein and W.H. Newell, 'Advancing Interdisciplinary
    Studies', in *Handbook of the Undergraduate Curriculum:
    A Comprehensive Guide to Purposes, Structures, Practices,
    and Change*, ed. by Jerry G. Gaff, James L. Ratcliff and
    Associates (San Francisco: Jossey-Bass, 1997), p.393.
5   'The Spectre of Interdisciplinarity,' *Dance Research
    Journal* 41:1 (2009), p.3.
6   Mark Franko, 'Editor's Note: Un-disciplined
    Questioning,' *Dance Research Journal* 41:1 (2009), p.vi.
7   Susanne Franco and Marina Nordera, 'Introduction,' in

Dance Discourses: Keywords in Dance Research (London: Routledge, 2007), p.2.

8   This tendency in the Sydney independent dance community and the conditions that have produced it were discussed at a symposium for the dance community held at the University of New South Wales with industry partner Performance Space on 7 April 2009; *Where is INDEPENDENT DANCE in Sydney?* For a report on this event, see Erin Brannigan, 'A Matter of Urgency,' *RealTime* no. 91 (June-July 2009), available online at http://www.realtimearts.net/article/issue91/9460 (accessed 26 July 2010).

9   For examples of this, and on their re-positioning of dance within their various fields of academic research, in addition to André Lepecki's above-cited *Exhausting Dance* (2006), see Andrew Hewitt, *Social Choreography: Ideology as Performance in Dance and Everyday Movement*, (Durham: Duke University Press, 2005); Erin Manning, *Politics of Touch: Sense, Movement, Sovereignty* (Minneapolis: University of Minnesota Press, 2007) and Carrie Lambert-Beatty, *Being Watched: Yvonne Rainer and the 1960s* (Cambridge, Mass.: MIT Press, 2008).

10   'Undisciplined subjects, unregulated practices: dancing in the academy,' in *Conference Proceedings: Dance Rebooted: Initializing the Grid*, ed. by Kim Vincs (Ausdance National, 2005), available at http://www.ausdance.org. au/resources/publications/dance-rebooted-initializing-the-grid/papers/Dempster.pdf (accessed 26 July 2010). This 'working paper' has helped me greatly in thinking through the question of disciplinarity in dance.

11   'Part I: Characteristics of the Modern Dance', in *The Modern Dance* (New York: Dance Horizons, 1972), pp.1–33.

12 Quoted in *The Dancer and the Dance: Merce Cunningham in conversation with Jacqueline Lesschaeve* (New York: Marion Boyars, 1991), p.139.

13 '"No" to Spectacle ...', in *The Routledge Dance Studies Reader*, ed. by Alexandra Carter (London: Routledge, 1998), p.35.

14 Simone Forti, 'Style is a Corset,' interview with Christophe Wavelet, *Writings on Dance: Constellations of Things*, 18/19 (1999), 147.

15 'Preface,' *Writings on Dance: Exploring the New Dance Aesthetic* 14 (1995/6), p.3 and 'Imagery, Ideokinesis and Choreography', *Writings on Dance: Ideokinesis and Dancemaking* 1 (1985), pp.18–19.

16 *Writings on Dance: Exploring the New Dance Aesthetic*, p.4. Other somatic practices currently used by contemporary dancers include Feldenkrais Method, contact improvisation, Bartenieff Fundamentals based on Rudolf von Laban's work, modern martial art forms such as Capoeira, and the Skinner Releasing Technique developed in the early 1960s by ex-Graham and Cunningham dancer, Joan Skinner.

17 *Exhausting Dance*, p.5.

18 'Thinking Dance,' in *What I Think about When I Think about Dancing*, exhibition catalogue, ed. by Lisa Havilah, Emma Saunders and Susan Gibb (Campbelltown: Campbelltown Arts Centre, 2009), p.103.

19 'Thinking Dance', p.104.

20 'Afterword,' *Lamb at the Altar: The Story of a Dance* (Durham: Duke University Press, 1994), pp.95–6.

21 Sally Gardner, 'Dancing with Russell Dumas: Some working notes,' *Writings on Dance: DIY? Ecologies of Practice* 21 (2001/2), 64.

22 The Ballets Russes criss-crossed with the newly emerging 'modern dance' in Western Europe, setting a

precedent for choreographic collaboration with avant-garde leaders in other fields, including Igor Stravinsky, Leon Bakst, Pablo Picasso and André Derain. Fuller added science and technology to dance, creating remarkable apparitions out of physical movement, silk fabrics and new stage-lighting techniques.

23 Wavelet 'Style is a Corset,' *Writings on Dance: Constellations of Things* 18/19 (1999), 151.

24 *Being Watched: Yvonne Rainer and the 1960s* (2008).

25 '*Scène* and contemporaneity,' trans. by Noémie Solomon, *TDR: The Drama Review* 51:2 (2007), pp.125–7.

26 '*Scène* and contemporaneity', pp.129–30.

27 Unless otherwise indicated, all the following quotations are taken from anonymously authored festival press material.

28 Maggi Phillips, 'Diversified Moves of a Specialised Ecology: Can This Art-Form be Sustainable?' in *Conference Proceedings: Dance Rebooted: Initializing the Grid* (Ausdance National, 2005), pp.9–10, available at http://www.ausdance.org.au/resources/publications/dance-rebooted-initializing-the-grid/papers/Phillips.pdf (accessed 26 July 2010).

29 Hilary Crampton, 'Redefining the Field—Expanding the Field,' in *Conference Proceedings: Dance Rebooted: Initializing the Grid* (Ausdance National, 2005), pp.1–4, available at http://www.ausdance.org.au/resources/publications/dance-rebooted-initializing-the-grid/papers/Crampton.pdf (accessed: 26 July 2010).

30 Sue Street, 'Reframing Arguments about the Value of Contemporary Dance: putting creativity at the centre of dance practice, policy and education,' Brolga 30 (2009), pp.7–8. Despite the title of this article, no creative artists are named with the exception of 'the great Australian choreographer Lloyd Newson,' whom

she cites in support of extended research periods for artists (p.5). This seems at odds with her call for wider participation and repeated references to *So You Think You Can Dance* which surely diffuse the kind of disciplined creative focus exemplified by Newson.

31 *Dance Discourses: Keywords in Dance Research* (London: Routledge, 2007), p.2.

32 Pouillaude p.127.

33 Interview with Grace Edwards for *Dance Informa*, posted 1 February 2010; available at http//:www.danceinforma.com/magazine/?p=2116 (accessed 31 August 2010).

34 Platform Paper, no. 8 (Sydney: Currency House, 2006).

35 'Undisciplined subjects, unregulated practices: dancing in the academy' (see n.10 above).

36 Elizabeth Dempster, 'Not Dancing under Modernism: Duncan and the Postmoderns,' *Writings on Dance* 24 (2007), p.49.

37 P.A.R.T.S Curriculum, available at http://www.parts.be/ (accessed 30 June 2010).

38 Unpublished report prepared for this essay.

39 Branch Nebula home page, at http//:members.iinet.net.au/-mirabellekes/ (accessed 31 August 2010).

40 Critical Path home page, at http//:www.criticalpath.org.au/about.html (accessed 31 August 2010).

41 'What I Think about When I Think about Dancing', in *What I Think about When I Think about Dancing*, p.12.

Readers' Forum

Response to Shilo McClean's *The Digital Playing Field: New Rulz for Films, Art and Performance*, (Platform Papers 24)

Augusta Supple is a director, playwright, musician and all-round stage practitioner who works in Australia and Canada. For the past four years she has created programs, panels and festivals to nurture and celebrate new Australian writing. This review was first published on 23 August on her website, http://augustasupple.com/

I've been carrying this Platform Paper around with me for a couple of months. It's only a slim book, so it hasn't been a great burden. There's just a lot for me to think about—and that's why I love it.

There's a row of Platform Papers in the bookcase in my office. They stand with black or brightly-coloured spines in rainbows on my shelf. Regardless of the date on the cover, they are a timeless contribution in my thinking about art, practice and culture. At times I have felt challenged or confronted by the papers—but mainly engaged and stimulated and I always look forward to seeing what comes next. On this occasion, a paper on digital storytelling by Dr Shilo McLean.

I first met Shilo when I was working at the then NSW Film and Television Office (now Screen NSW—a telling transformation as the industry shifts from 'film' to 'screen', don't you think?). I had always considered Shilo's interests in digital media/effects and my own practice in theatre as utterly opposed. In fact, I found myself cringing, repelled by the idea that the theatre could be usurped by cyborg avatars—Amazonian women and rippling men whose flesh-selves were pale, anti-social nerds hunched over a mouse or control pad, pecking away at a keyboard as blue light cast shadows of flickering action over a cluttered bedroom. My fear that reality would be substituted by fantasy: that the digital would ultimately be more satisfying to the general public than a live event—lingered. My life's passion and work in the theatre trampled by a storm-trooping digital boot attached to the impossible thigh of a woman I could never hope to look like. The fear—huge; and upon reading Shilo's paper—ridiculous.

Strange that I should not make the correlation with Sontag's writings, especially Plato's Cave. Strange that I felt threatened by the solitary image of someone huddled at a computer screen making stories. Theatre is ultimately a collaborative art form: its makers are making in real time with each other. I had forgotten that in theatre, though we may be sitting in an audience collectively experiencing a live event, ultimately we are still alone with our unique experience of that event. Strange that a topic such as digital media should be bound in the seemingly antique tradition of a paperback book. Strange that I, a theatre practitioner and occasional reviewer, so easily engages with an online site (web log). Strange how the innovative and unusual become the focal point of fear, then of acceptance, then common exploitation. The internet, once the reserve of the rich and nerdy, is now, in our Western culture, an assumed right. Strange that my fear made me ignorant of the skills and devices, the ethics and the issues, the possibilities and the practices of this new tool. Strange that I had never acknowledged how much digital tools have freed and assisted my thinking, my engagement with the arts, with my own practice. As Shilo states:

> There is something about art and performance that draws upon our fears, and perhaps this is what incites our desire to control, to regulate to mediate and yes, to censor. Whatever the medium, be it images, live performance or literary narrative, the aim is the expression and communication of emotions and ideas. (p.4)

A relief that Currency House has commissioned this paper from McClean, to drag me out of an ignorant, quivering fear and into the light.

McClean tracks the development of digital tools through filmmaking, addresses the nay-sayers, the critics, the conservatives, the censors and the content taste-makers. She speaks of storytelling as 'one of the cleverest, most important things we analogue creatures do... [which is a] means of passing on knowledge and wisdom'. She talks of the technological revolution which put professional-level equipment in the hands of novices and created a DIY culture of creation and a culture of identity-creation... whereby people are actively engaging in creating stories and being a part of the mythology of the story through its gaming incantations, through the creation of their own versions of their favourite films, by creating T-Shirts online etc. She writes of the blurring of the professional and the amateur, of the independent filmmaker and what access to equipment and technology has done to the creation of art. It is a fascinating book which references the hybridisation of storytelling—the audience as maker—and the potential of audiences to be highly-involved and creatively-evolved participants in creation. She talks about the role of censorship in art, in copyright issues surrounding sampling, and mash-ups... she talks about the politics of broadband access, usage... It's a thoroughly engaging and rollicking read—even if it is in ye olde format of paper and stitch-binding.

Subscribe to **Platform Papers**

Have the papers delivered quarterly to your door

4 issues for $60.00 including postage within Australia

The individual recommended retail price is $14.95.

___ I would like to subscribe to 4 issues of Platform Papers for $60.00

I would like my subscription to start from: ___ this issue (No. 25)

___ the next issue (No. 26)

Name_____

Address_____

_____

_____ State _____ Postcode _____

Email _____

Telephone _____

Please make cheques payable to Currency House Inc.

Or charge: ___ Mastercard ___ Visa

Card no. ___ ___ ___ ___ ___ ___ ___ ___ ___ ___ ___ ___

___ ___ ___ ___

Expiry date _____ Signature _____

CURRENCY HOUSE

Fax this form to Currency House Inc. at: 02 9319 3649

Or post to: Currency House Inc., PO Box 2270, Strawberry Hills NSW 2012 Australia